BUILD YOUR OWN
DINOSAURS

By Dennis Schatz   Illustrations by Bob Greisen

Andrews and McMeel

A Universal Press Syndicate Company

Kansas City

Build Your Own Dinosaurs copyright © 1994 by becker&mayer!, Ltd. All rights reserved. Printed in Hong Kong. No part of this book may be used or reproduced in any manner whatsoever without written permission except in the case of reprints in the context of reviews. For information, write Andrews and McMeel, a Universal Press Syndicate Company, 4900 Main Street, Kansas City, Missouri 64112.

From the Build Your Own Dinosaurs packaged set, which includes rubber stamps, ink pad, and this book.

ISBN: 0-8362-4512-1

Library of Congress Catalog Card Number: 94-70001

The Build Your Own Dinosaurs packaged set is produced by becker&mayer!, Ltd.
Rubber-stamp illustrations by Sylvia Oltion Shapiro
Design and illustration for cover and package by Peter Georgeson
Composition by Dona McAdam, Mac on the Hill

To Andy and Jim who inspired the concept for this book.

Other children's kits from
Andrews and McMeel by becker&mayer!
The Amazing Sandcastle Builder's Kit
The Ant Book & See-Through Model
The American Appaloosa
The English Thoroughbred
Fun with Ballet
Fun with Electronics
Sleeping Beauty

A Note about Your Dinosaur Rubber Stamps

In the stamp box, you will find a pre-printed sheet of 24 stickers for all of the stamps in this kit. Before using them for the first time, attach the correct sticker to the back of each stamp.

With these stamps you can make seven different dinosaurs. To stamp out a dinosaur skeleton, follow the "dinosaur blueprints" that appear in this book. Don't worry if your dinosaur doesn't look exactly like the blueprint. Nobody knows exactly what the dinosaurs looked like—so your version might be just right!

Dinosaurs were the largest land animals ever to live, though not all of them were huge. Some were larger than a school bus. Others were only the size of a chicken.

The first dinosaurs lived on the earth 225 million years ago. If we could travel back in time so that each year passed in one second, it would take more than seven years to get back to when the dinosaurs first lived on the earth. Not every kind of dinosaur lived at the same time. Each type could be found on the earth for a five- to twenty-million-year period, and individual dinosaurs probably lived fifty to one hundred years, much like large mammals or reptiles of today.

Dinosaurs lived on the earth for 160 million years, much longer than the two to four million years that humans have existed so far. The last of the dinosaurs died around sixty-five million years ago.

We know about animals that lived so long ago because on rare occasions mud or sand covered their bodies when they died. The skin and other soft parts of their bodies decayed, but over millions of years the bones slowly turned to stone. These stones are called fossils.

Scientists known as paleontologists uncover these fossils in dinosaur digs around the world. Paleontologists rarely find fossils of whole dinosaur skeletons. They usually find just a few bones. If many bones are found, they are typically scattered over a large area, making it difficult to know how the bones were once attached to each other.

Paleontologists know how different bones fit together from studying animals that are alive today. They use this information to assemble the fossils into an entire dinosaur skeleton. These skeletons are displayed in museums around the world.

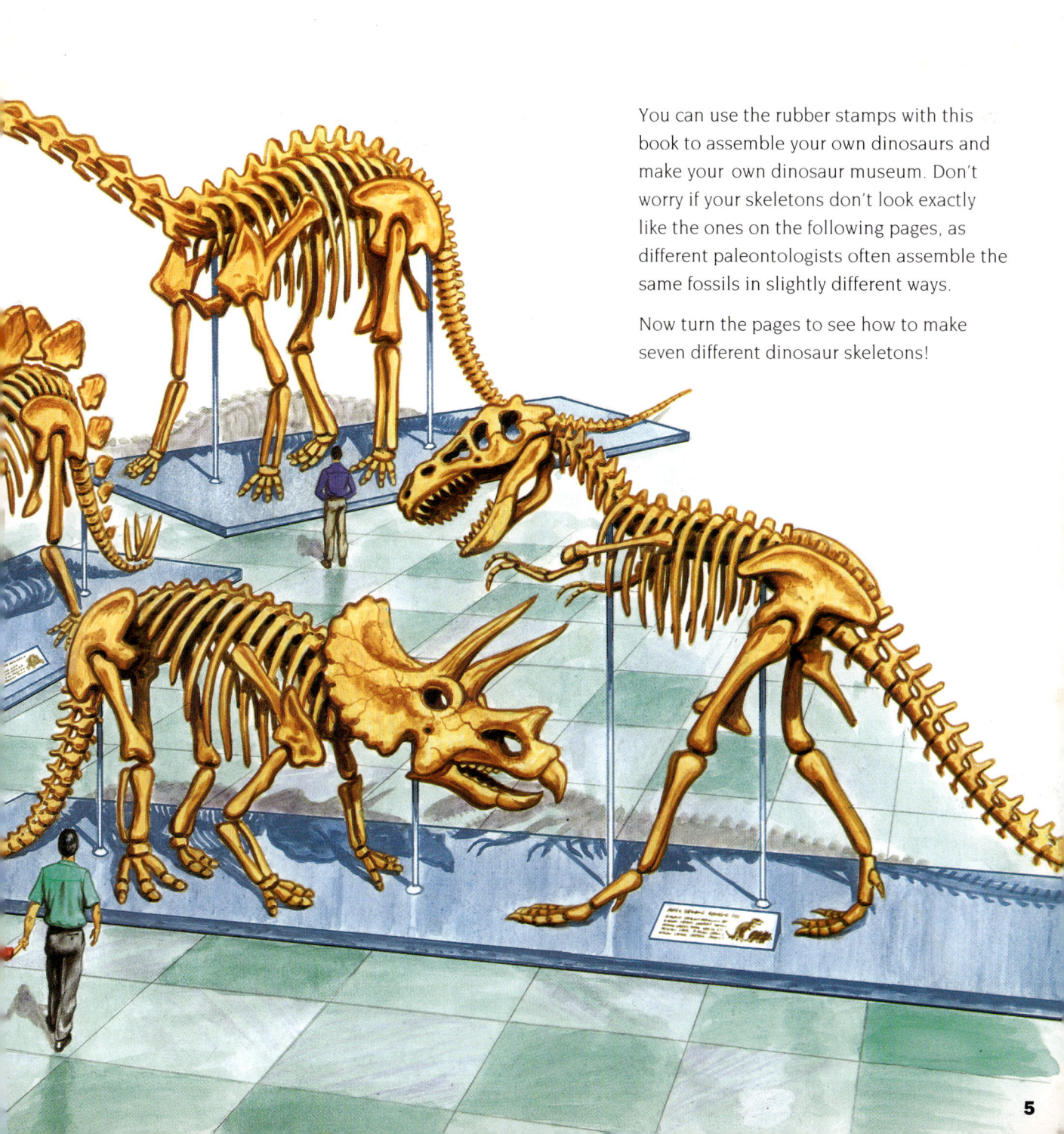

You can use the rubber stamps with this book to assemble your own dinosaurs and make your own dinosaur museum. Don't worry if your skeletons don't look exactly like the ones on the following pages, as different paleontologists often assemble the same fossils in slightly different ways.

Now turn the pages to see how to make seven different dinosaur skeletons!

TYRANNOSAURUS REX (tyrant lizard king)

Tyrannosaurus rex (ty-RAN-uh-SAWR-us rex) dinosaurs lived about seventy million years ago. It was the largest of the meat-eating dinosaurs, weighing over 10,000 pounds and measuring more than forty feet long—about the size and weight of a small school bus. Its seven-inch-long curved teeth had special ridges, much like those on a steak knife, to cut through the thick skin of its prey. The teeth curved backward so that any prey trying to escape would push the teeth farther into its body.

This "king of the dinosaurs" walked on two legs. Each foot had three claws in front—similar to those of modern-day birds—and one pointing to the back. The front legs were extremely short and had two small claws at the end. The use for these unusually small front legs will probably remain a mystery. They could not reach the dinosaur's mouth and so were not used for feeding. They were too small to be of any use in killing prey. One possibility is that these legs helped the dinosaur get up when it was lying down.

Tyrannosaurus rex's long tail counterbalanced its large head. Built like a football running-back, this massive animal could change directions quickly and run up to forty-five miles per hour.

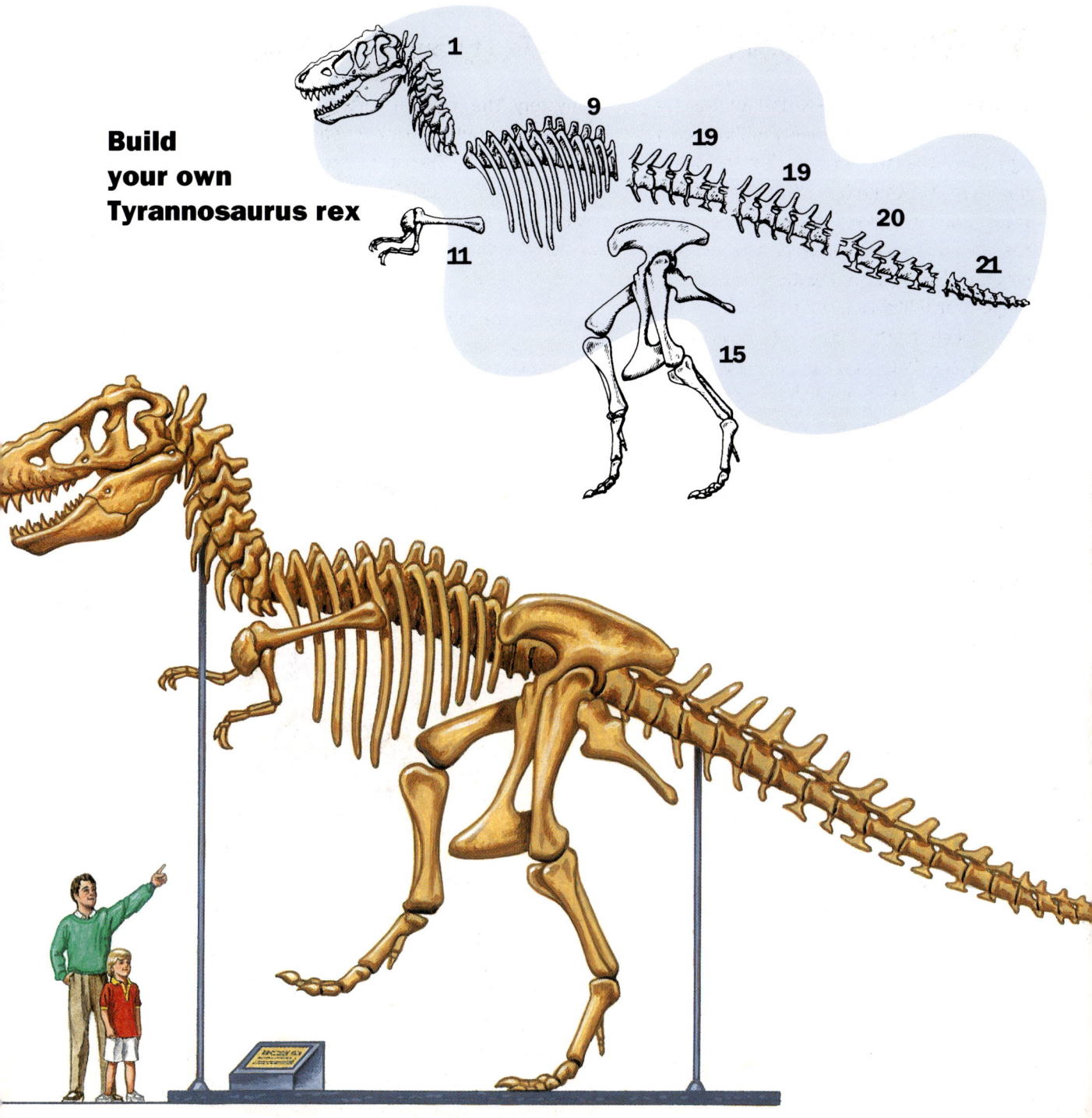

VELOCIRAPTOR (swift plunderer)

Velociraptor (veh-loss-ih-RAP-tor) dinosaurs lived about seventy-five million years ago and were only six feet tall. Velociraptor probably hunted in packs to kill large dinosaurs. The ten-inch-long claw on each back foot was well adapted for hunting. A special hinge at the base of the claw rotated it out of the way for walking, but also allowed the claw to move in a wide arc to cut though the skin of its prey.

Velociraptor's front claws acted like hooks to cling to its prey while the rear claws sliced it open.

Velociraptor had a slender, sharply curved neck that gave it a large range of movements. Its tail counterbalanced its head to make the dinosaur quick and agile.

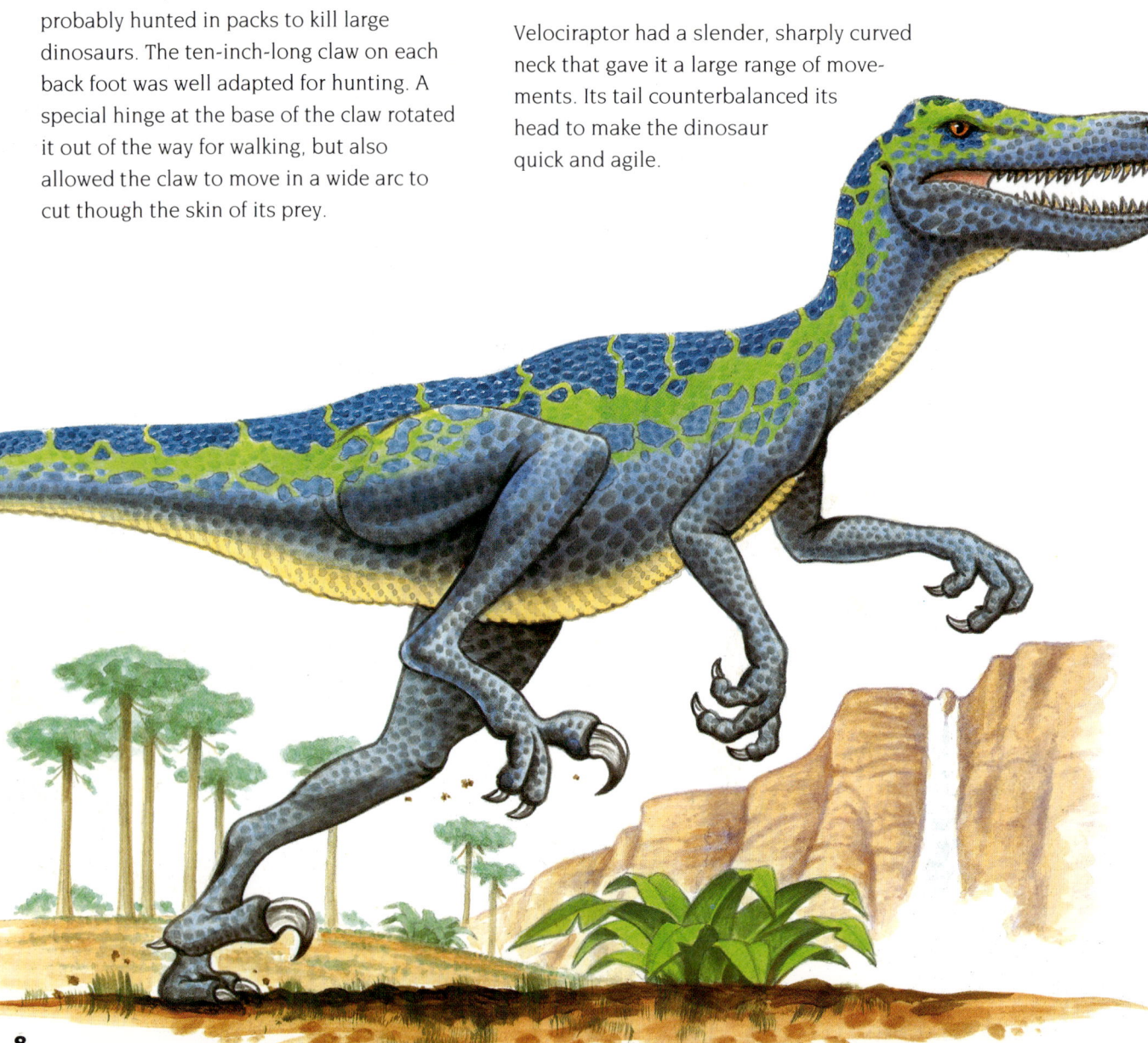

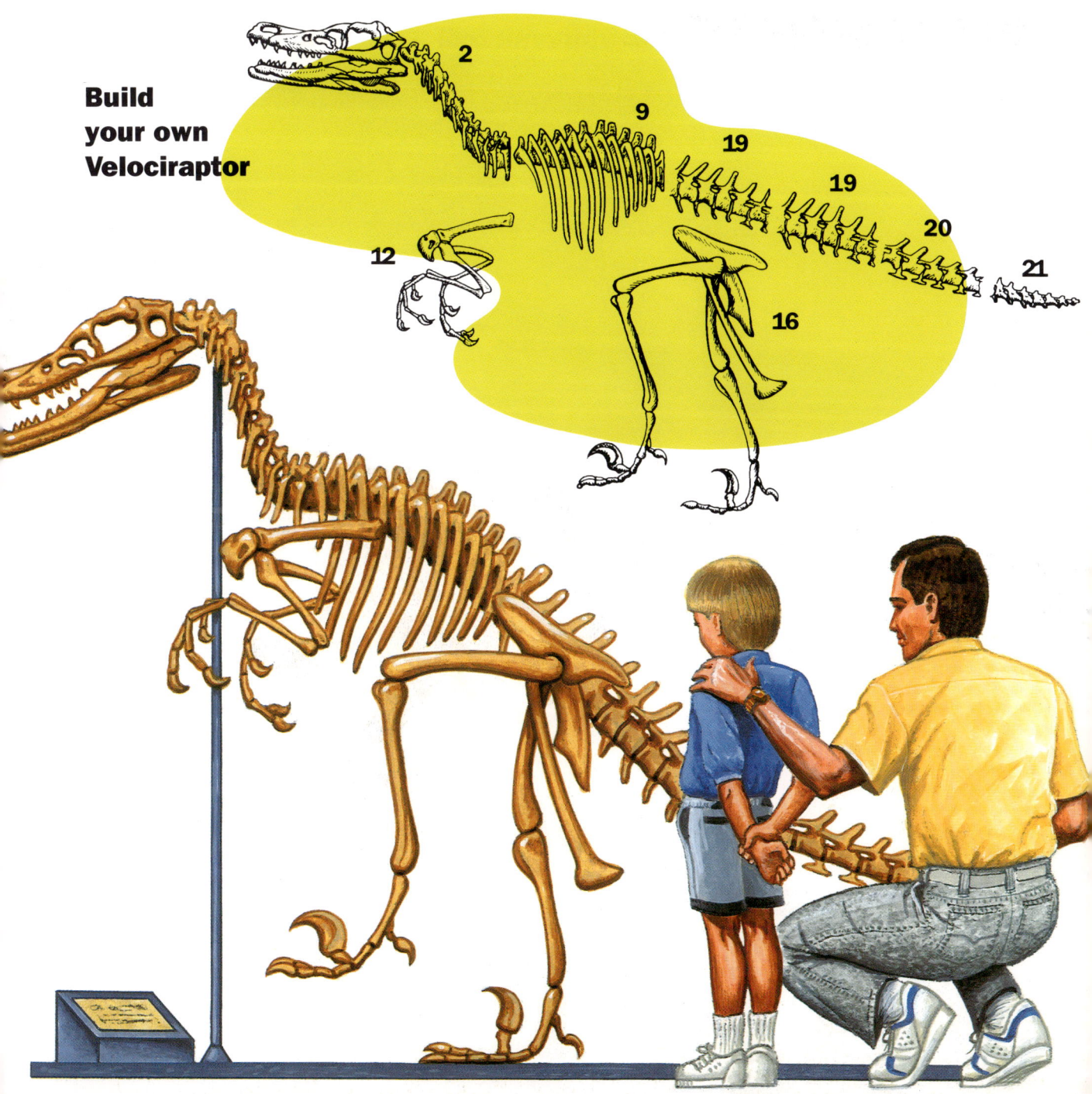

APATOSAURUS (deceptive lizard)

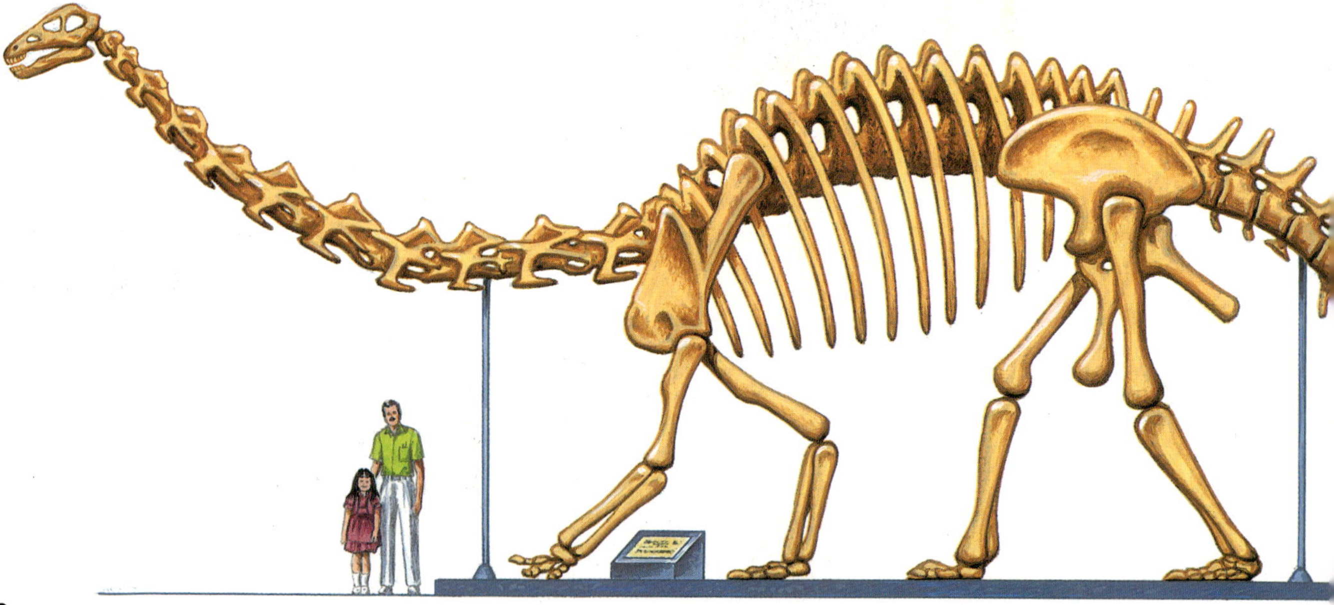

Apatosaurus (ah-PAT-uh-SAUR-us) dinosaurs lived about 170 million years ago. They grew to sixty-five feet long and weighed over 50,000 pounds—almost as long and heavy as a fully loaded semitrailer. Its long neck helped reach vegetation in tall trees.

Unlike most plant-eaters, Apatosaurus did not have large flat teeth in the back of its mouth for chewing what it ate. Instead, at the front of its mouth it had peg-like teeth that showed little wear. Paleontologists think that Apatosaurus used its teeth to bite off plants and then swallowed them whole. The dinosaur's stomach contained large stones that the dinosaur had swallowed earlier, which helped grind up the plants much the same way that the stones in a bird's gizzard help them digest seeds.

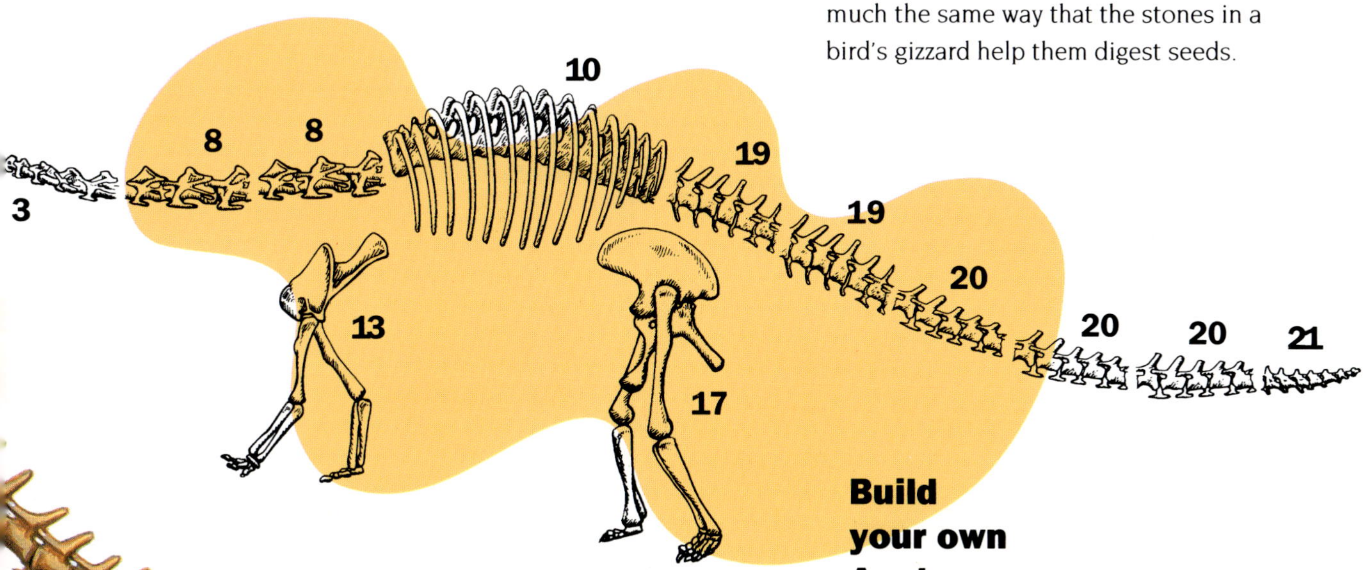

Build your own Apatosaurus

STEGOSAURUS
(plated lizard)

Stegosaurus (STEG-uh-SAWR-us) dinosaurs lived about 150 million years ago. They were about thirty feet long and weighed up to 4,000 pounds.

Paleontologists used to think that the large plates along the dinosaur's back provided protection from meat-eating dinosaurs. Recent studies of the fossils show that many blood vessels ran along the plates, which would not be true if the plates were for protection. Most scientists now think that the plates were solar collectors that helped control the animal's temperature. Turning the plates toward or away from the sun allowed Stegosaurus to heat or cool its blood to keep its body at the right temperature.

The animal's primary means of defense were the large spikes at the end of its tail, which it could swing with great force against an attacking enemy.

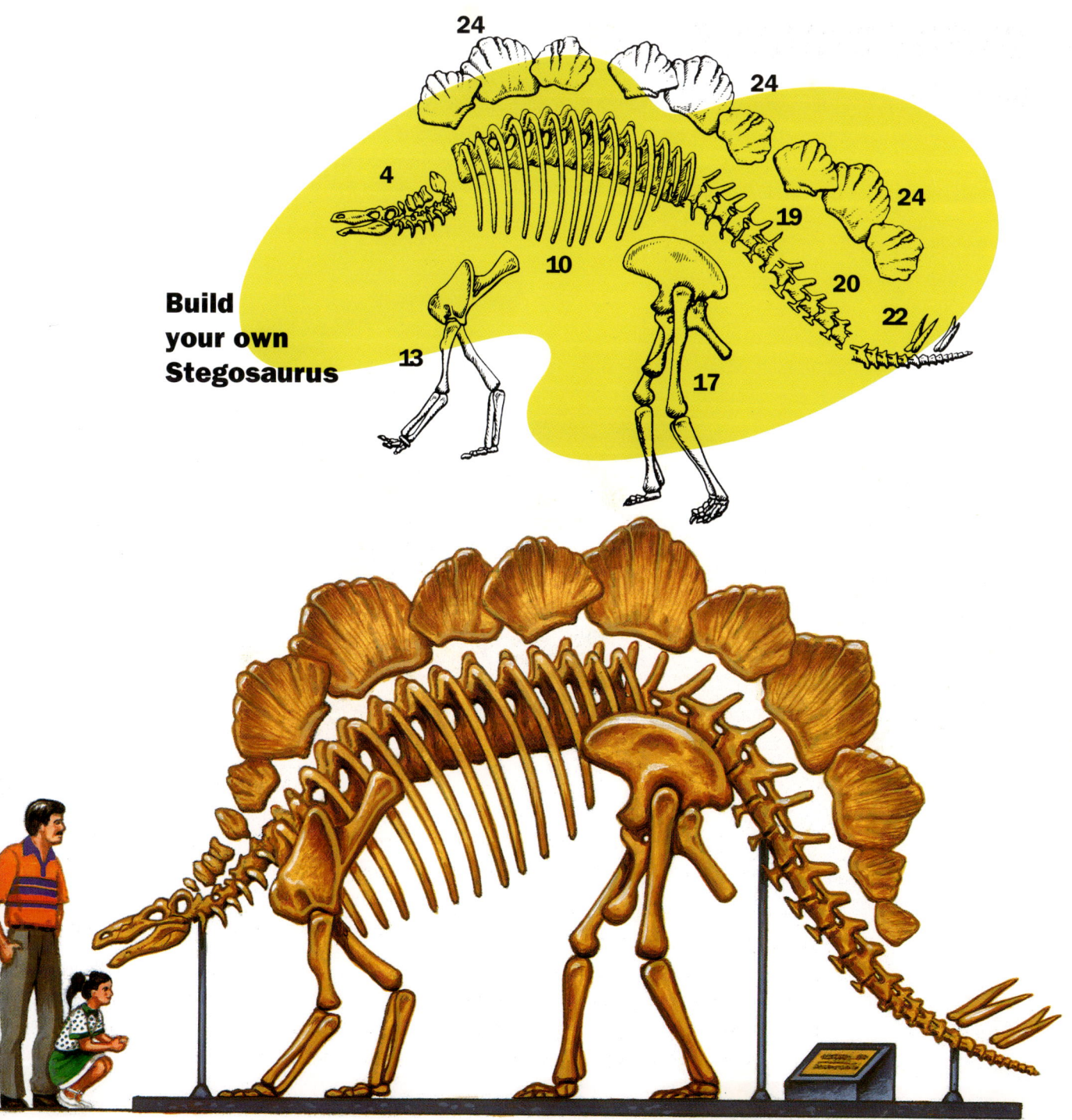

PARASAUROLOPHUS (two-ridged lizard)

Parasaurolophus (par-uh-sawr-OL-uh-fus) dinosaurs lived about seventy-five million years ago. They were about thirty feet long and had the most elaborate skull structure of any of the dinosaurs. The three-foot-long horn was actually a long tube that connected to the animal's nose. When Parasaurolophus blew into the tube, it made a loud, distinctive, trombone-like noise. This noise probably sent a warning to other animals or possibly attracted a mate.

Parasaurolophus was one type of "duckbill" dinosaur. The front of its mouth had no teeth, but contained a bony ridge similar to that of a duck. It effectively snipped off vegetation that was transferred to the back of its mouth for thorough grinding by strong molar teeth.

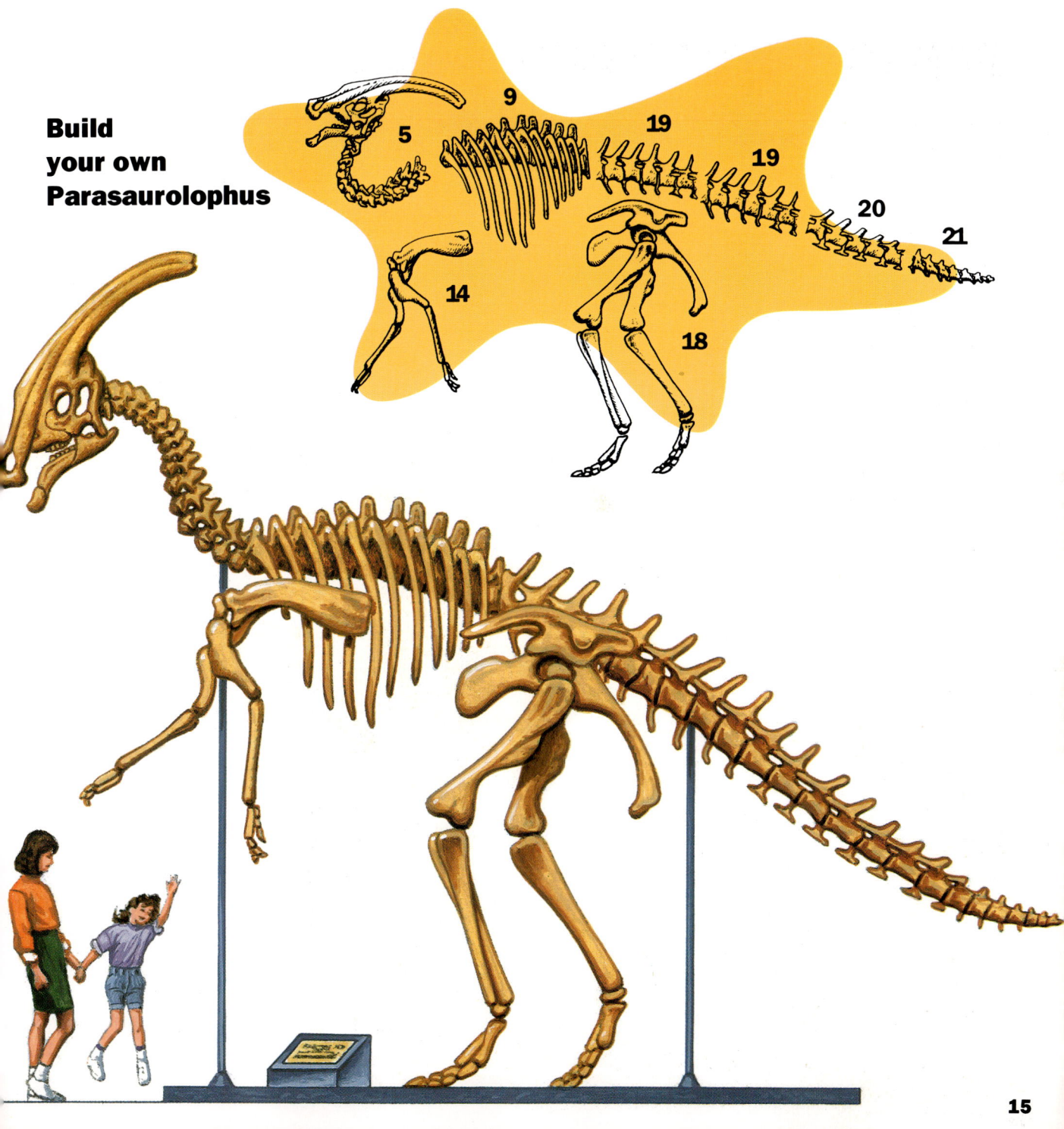
Build your own Parasaurolophus

TRICERATOPS (three-horned face)

Triceratops (try-SAIR-uh-tops) dinosaurs lived about seventy million years ago. They were around thirty feet long and weighed as much as 18,000 pounds. The large bony shield, called a frill, on the back of the massive head probably protected the dinosaur's vulnerable neck from predators or helped attract a mate. The frill also provided a strong anchor for the massive jaw muscles, which connected to a sharp beak. This beak let Triceratops bite through the toughest branches before transferring the plant material to large molar teeth for thorough grinding.

Built like a rhinoceros, Triceratops charged other animals to defend itself. The head—up to eight feet long—was finely balanced so Triceratops could easily attack other animals with its three long horns, which were as long as four feet.

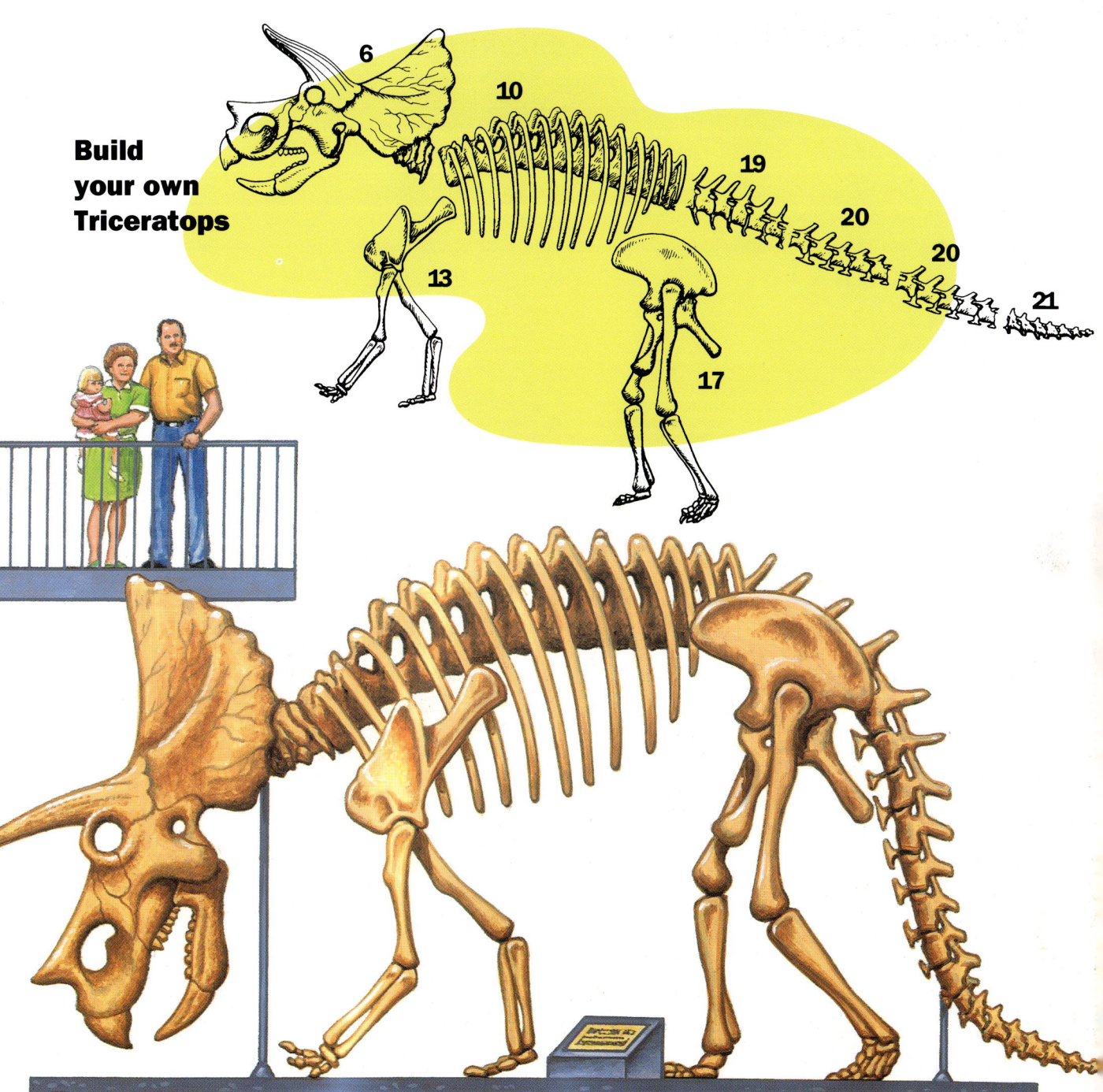

Build your own Triceratops

ANKYLOSAURUS (fused lizard)

Ankylosaurus (AN-ki-luh-SAWR-us) dinosaurs lived around seventy million years ago. They were about thirty feet long and weighed up to 8,000 pounds. The bony plates, knobs, and horns that covered the top of its body—even its eyelids—protected Ankylosaurus against meat-eating dinosaurs.

Ankylosaurus would crouch low to the ground when attacked in order to protect its soft underside, at the same time presenting to the attacker an impregnable shield of bony plates on its back. A large club at the end of its tail delivered a strong blow to disable or trip the attacker.

Build your own Ankylosaurus

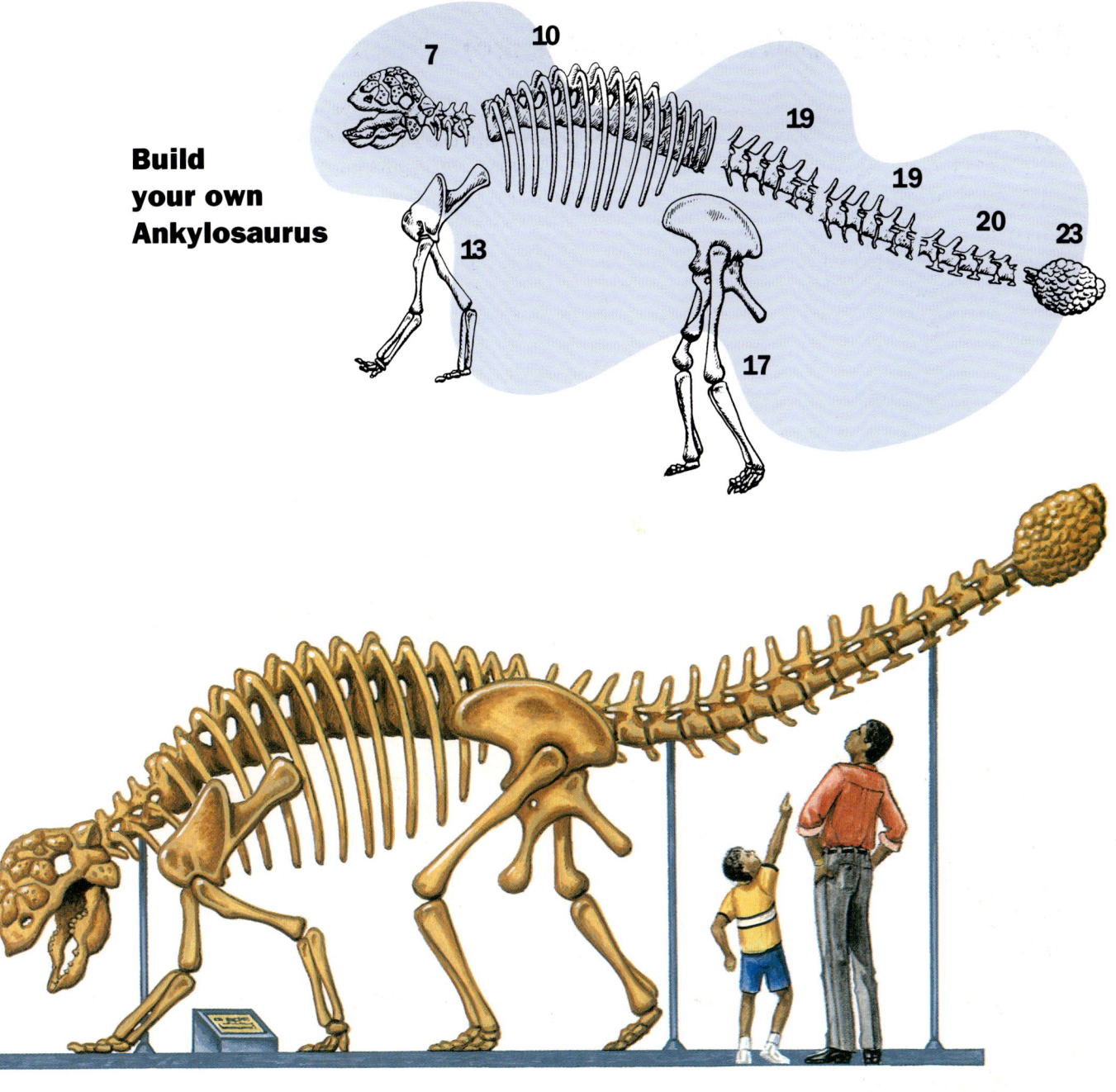

After living for 160 million years, the dinosaurs disappeared from the Earth. Paleontologists have several ideas about what may have caused the dinosaurs to become extinct:

- The climate may have changed so quickly that the dinosaurs could not adapt. Individual plants today experience something similar when they are killed by the first days of frost. These plants would become extinct if they did not have seeds that survived the winter and grew again in the spring.

- The dinosaurs traveled long distances to find new sources of food and water. On these travels they may have exchanged diseases with other animals that caused all the dinosaurs to die. This is similar to what happened when early human explorers traveled to new lands. Many native people and explorers died from sicknesses they experienced for the first time.

- The most widely accepted idea for why the dinosaurs became extinct is that an asteroid or meteorite (a large rock) or a comet (a rocky snowball) collided with the earth. This produced a large explosion and started forest fires that threw tons of rock, dust, and ash into the air. This material completely covered the earth and blocked out the sun. With less sunlight reaching the surface of the earth, many of the plants and animals could not survive.

Whatever the reason for the dinosaur's extinction, it happened quickly and ultimately to the benefit of humans. The dinosaurs so dominated the Earth that if they had continued to live, mammals (including you and me) probably would not have spread across the Earth—and you would not be reading this book today!

Determining how a dinosaur looked begins with digging up bones in the fossil field. Bulldozers, jackhammers, pickaxes, shovels, and brooms remove the dirt and rock from the area around the fossils. Removing the rock right next to the fossils requires delicate work with hand chisels, dental drills, tweezers, and brushes.

Fossils often crack or break when uncovered, so they are wrapped in burlap cloth soaked in plaster of paris. The plaster holds the fossil together for shipping to the laboratory, just like a cast on a broken arm holds the bones together until they heal.

Paleontologists are uncovering the fossils of a Stegosaurus in this dig. See if you can match some of these fossils with your rubber-stamp skeletons.

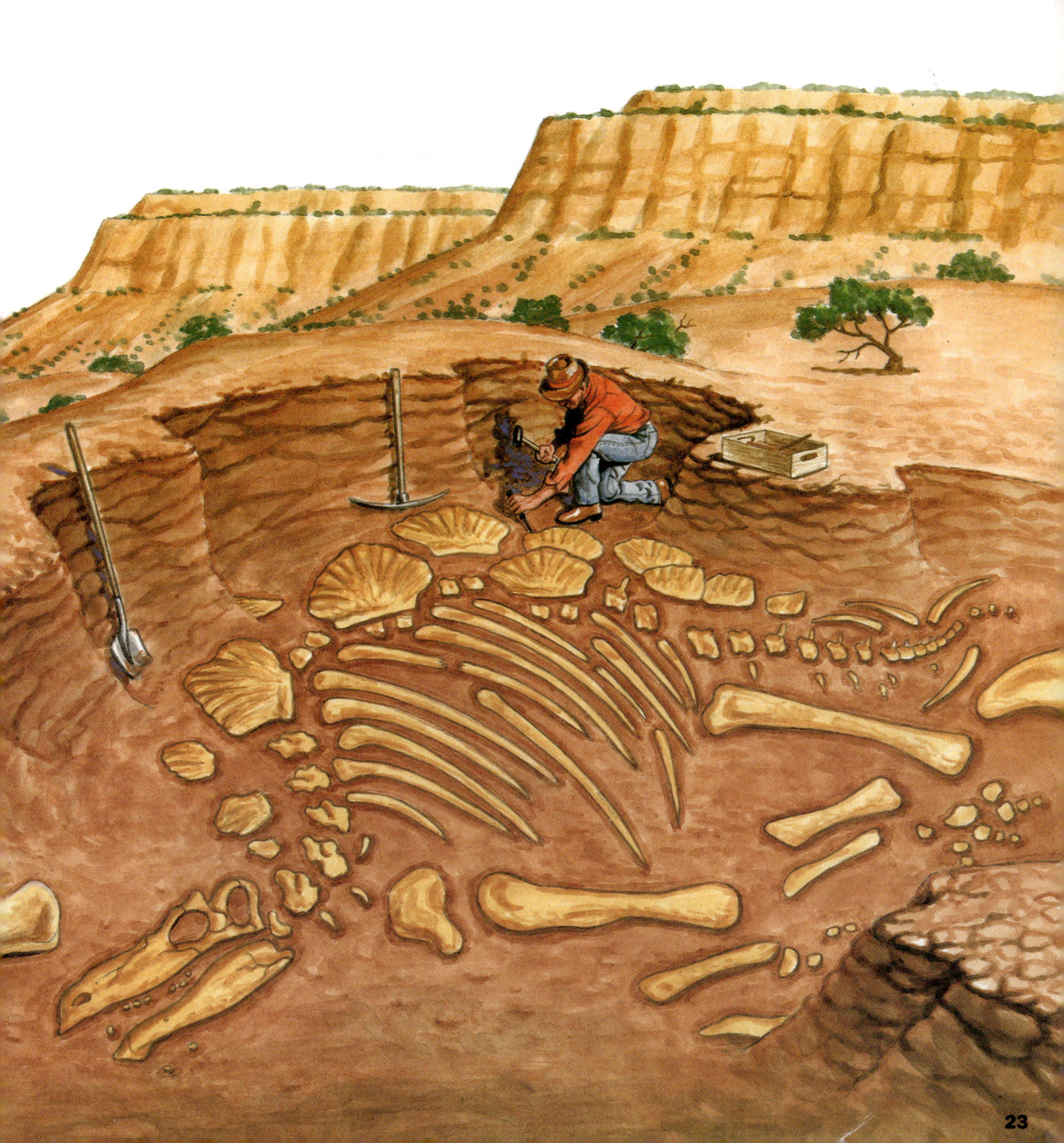

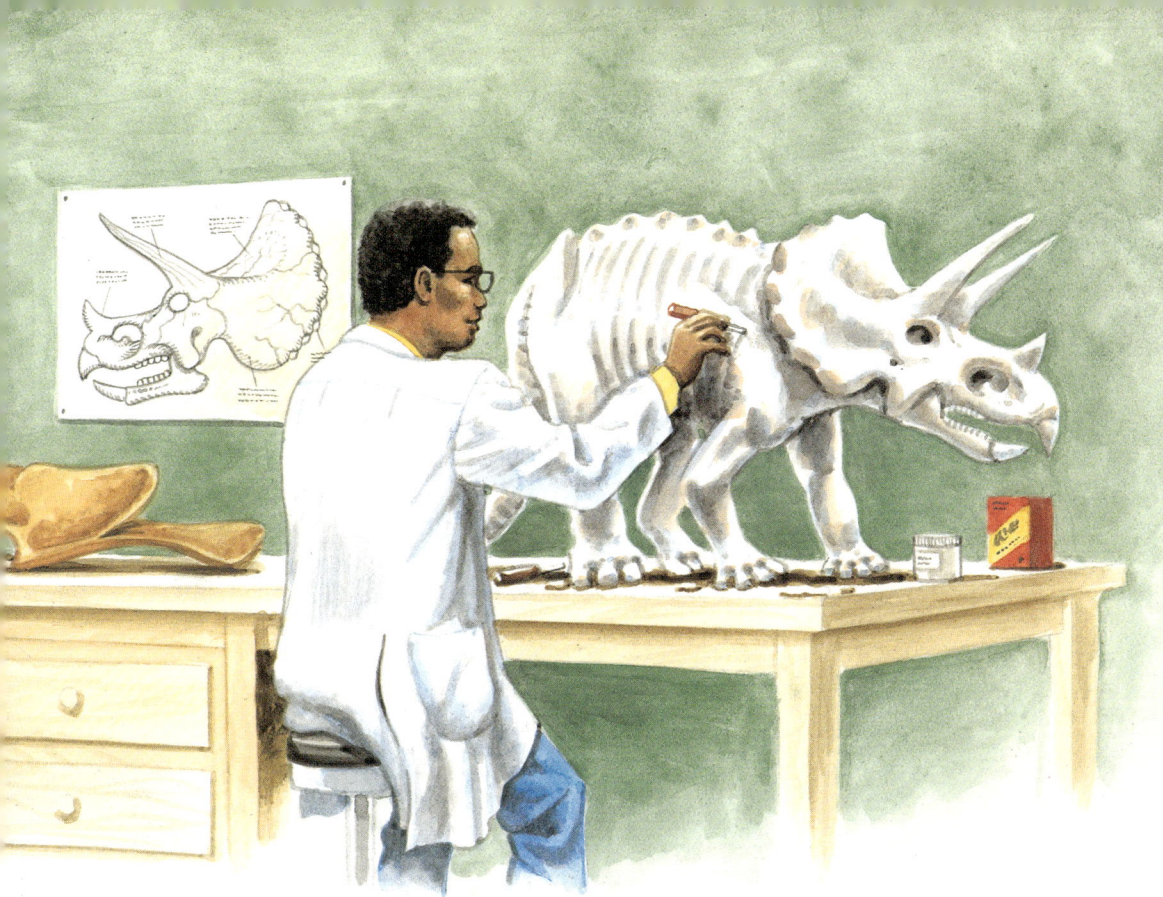

Most people think of paleontologists as people who spend most of their time digging up fossils, but most of the work occurs in the paleontologist's laboratory at a university or museum. A paleontologist generally spends the summer digging up fossils and the rest of the year in the laboratory cleaning and studying them.

In the laboratory the fossils are separated from the plaster and surrounding rock. The size and shape of the bones are compared to today's animals. This information is used to determine how the bones connect as well as how the dinosaur moved, how it ate, and what it ate.

Modern equipment used in medicine, such as X-ray machines, show the microscopic details of dinosaur bone structure. This type of information helps answer one of the major questions about dinosaurs: Were the dinosaurs cold-blooded or warm-blooded?

For a long time, paleontologists thought that the dinosaur was a cold-blooded animal, meaning its temperature is the same as its surroundings. If it wants to get warmer, it simply moves into the sun. If it needs to cool off, it moves into the shade. As its temperature goes down, so does its activity. A cold-blooded animal requires less food than a warm-blooded animal, because it does not have to use energy to keep its body at the same temperature the way a warm-blooded animal does. The cold-blooded snake only needs to eat once a week while the warm-blooded bird needs to eat daily.

Today, most scientists believe that the dinosaurs were actually warm-blooded because:

- Dinosaurs evolved into birds, which are warm-blooded.

- Most dinosaurs had strong teeth or stomach stones, which allowed them to eat enough food to support a warm-blooded existence.

- Dinosaur bones viewed through a microscope show numerous blood vessels and growth rates similar to those of modern warm-blooded animals.

Many museum exhibits display dinosaurs in settings that emphasize the active nature of warm-blooded animals. These exhibits often show how the different dinosaurs interacted.

To create your own museum exhibit, stamp out a dinosaur in the center of a piece of paper. Cut around the skeleton, making sure to leave about two inches of extra paper at the bottom. Fold over the extra paper so the dinosaur can stand upright. Repeat with more dinosaurs.

Now you can create a museum exhibit to show individual dinosaurs, herds of dinosaurs, or even meat-eating dinosaurs chasing plant-eating dinosaurs.